SELF
INQUIRY

SELF
INQUIRY

M. Robert Gardner

An Atlantic Monthly Press Book

Little, Brown and Company   Boston/Toronto

FIRST EDITION

Library of Congress Cataloging in Publication Data
Gardner, M. Robert.
 Self inquiry.
 "An Atlantic Monthly Press book."
 1. Self-actualization (Psychology) 2. Self-
realization. I. Title.
BF637.S4G37 1983 158'.1 83-9869
ISBN 0-316-30388-7

ATLANTIC–LITTLE, BROWN BOOKS
ARE PUBLISHED BY
LITTLE, BROWN AND COMPANY
IN ASSOCIATION WITH
THE ATLANTIC MONTHLY PRESS

BP

Designed by Dede Cummings

*Published simultaneously in Canada
by Little, Brown & Company (Canada) Limited*

PRINTED IN THE UNITED STATES OF AMERICA

To my patients and other teachers

The field that you are standing before appears to have the same proportions as your own life.

JOHN BERGER
About Looking

Preface

IN Patagonia they say: "Those who take credit for the sunshine must also take blame for the rain."

I cannot bring myself to lay that burden on all who have shaped my views, but neither can I resist thanking especially my wife, Elizabeth, my daughter, Lyn, my son, Peter, and my friends John Gedo, Lee Halprin, and Alain Schuster. They have helped me to find what I believe and to face the trials of an old talker trying to become a young writer.

Though I wrote these pages — or rather, the bulk of them — under Cambridge elms, on Cape Cod sands, and overlooking Paris rooftops, they bear the marks of a busman's holiday. They are my self inquiry into self inquiry and into psychoanalysis as an instance.

Having tried to swap words of my trade for more private words, and the comforts and aches of anonymity for those of the first-person singular, I feel like the patient who told me that till she was four she never talked, and once she talked, never stopped. If I talk too much now, I trust you will understand.

In Pursuit
of Psychoanalysis

P SYCHOANALYSTS fritter away large chances in half-truths. Psychoanalysts ape the forms and foul the spirit of yesterday's classics and of today's revolutions. Psychoanalysts are beset by orthodoxies of the right, orthodoxies of the left, and orthodoxies of the middle of the road.

Psychoanalysts try to prove themselves and psychoanalysis "classical" or prove themselves and psychoanalysis "not classical." What is "classical"? Pure? What is "not classical"? Impure? Popular? Purer than pure?

Psychoanalysts say: "I know this sounds classical, but . . ." They say: "I know this does not sound classical, but . . ." What is all this concern for how things sound? What are all these buts?

Adventure is perverted to debenture. Exploration gives way to oughts and shoulds. We *ought* to psychoanalyze this. We *ought* to psychoanalyze that. A good psychoanalyst *always* psychoanalyzes this before that, *always* does this or does that. A good psychoanalyst has good psychoanalytic hours, good psychoanalyses, and good patients. Can such pervasive talk of oughts, of shoulds, and of goods really be good?

Psychoanalysts boast of practicing X rather than X-1 or X-2 hours a day. And they boast of practicing X-1 or X-2 rather than X hours a day. What are we coming to? Should the carpenter boast that he hammered and sawed all day? Or that he did not hammer and saw all day?

Psychoanalysts talk of "suitable" and of "unsuitable" patients. What have we come to when it no longer seems bizarre to talk as if the method is what counts and the patient either fits or is a misfit? Mechanical gears rattle and creak where mechanical gears have no place.

And psychoanalysts try mechanically not to be mechanical. They try to show they are human. How can we *show* we are human? Either we are human or we are not. We are human enough in some ways, not human enough in others. Will a smile change that? A favor? A confession of faults? A folksy manner? Or what? And if psychoanalysis requires a "holding environment," will we try to make it more "holding"? If some is helpful, is more better? If the spontaneous is helpful, is forced better? If empathy, hope, and compassion count, will we make psychoanalysis into empathy, hope, and compassion therapy? Will we try to be latter-day good-enough mothers? If separation

4

counts, will we make psychoanalysis separation therapy? A "chance to grieve"? If "facing facts" counts, will we make psychoanalysis one long look at the "facts"? "Optimal disillusionment"? A blow to "entitlement"? A look at "reality"? If reliving and revising things past counts, will we define psychoanalysis as reliving and revising things past therapy? Must we pounce on anachronism as a hawk upon its prey? If we and our patients need an "alliance," must we make psycho-analysis read like a chapter of *How to Win Friends and Influence People* or like a tract from the Salvation Army? Will we and our patient be more "we" if we cling to the habit of saying "we" — whether we feel "we" or not? "And how are we this morning, Mrs. Smith?" Has it come to that?

Psychoanalysts push pat explanations for the com-plexity of the individual, and for the complexity of large social events — love, hate, work, play, art, sports, politics, crime, war and peace — and only tomorrow knows what else.

Afflicted with au-courant-ism, we confuse science with scientism. We play follow the leader and turn a brave method of inquiry into a timid tracing of obliga-tory topics.

Psychoanalysis so mauled and so mangled stops being inquiry and becomes a faddish search, a balanced survey course of previously discovered and categorized ideas, aims, feelings, events, complexes, urges, fears, defenses, transferences, resistances, disorders, arrests, stages, phases, and assorted etceteras. Powerful insights with fresh possibilities are cheapened into laundry lists of items to be identified and checked off. Love of inquiry, the act of inquiry, and the growth of the ability to inquire are sacrificed to a false reverence for particulars to be inquired into.

These unhappy ways testify not only to a failure of psychoanalysts to practice the self inquiry they preach, but to a failure to overcome the compulsion to name, the mania to manage, and the furor to cure, all of which, in our darkest hours, embrace the madness of believing that by treating someone as less than a person we can help him or her to become more of a person.

But who are "we"? Who are the psychoanalysts who do these things? Some do many of them all the time. All do some of them some of the time. At least, all I know. We want to be one way, and we find we are, over and over, despite our best efforts, exactly the opposite.

If I am talking about the occupational hazards not only of being a psychoanalyst but of being alive — I think I am talking of both — I refuse to drown my indignation in a sea of platitudes about human frailty. I mean to take these matters seriously. I mean to sacrifice the luxury of railing at "us" to the necessity of looking closer to home. I want to look at what I hope psychoanalysis to be and what I hope to be when I do what I hope to be psychoanalysis. I mean to find a way to think about self inquiry, my patient's and my own, so I may do more of what I hope and less of what I regret.

The first psychoanalyst found what most had failed to see, feared to see, and refused to see. He found disavowed purposes, and he found disavowed purposes for disavowing purposes. Finding these in himself helped him to find these in others/helped him to find these in himself. He used whatever genius he had for self inquiry to help others use whatever genius they had, and whatever genius others had to help him use whatever he had. These were large steps in the advance of self inquiry, his own and others'.

We can regard such advances as the rare possibilities of an unusually large talent or as the ongoing possibilities of the rest of us. We can leave the advances to Freud in the glow of his golden era of creativity, or we can claim the challenge and the chances for ourselves. Mainly we do better, I think, when knowingly or not — and better when knowingly than not — we do the latter rather than the former. I want at least to see where we are taken and where we can take it when we pursue the idea that the psychoanalyst's main aim, now as in Freud's time, is, or might well be, to advance his or her own self inquiry to help his or her patients to advance their self inquiry to help him or her to advance his or hers. And so on. And so on.

In this spirit, let me frame the assumptions in this set of assertions:

Departures from the ideal notwithstanding, the pursuit of psychoanalysis is the pursuit of two self inquiries. If the aim is simple, the carrying out is not. Every patient and every psychoanalyst, the first and each after, has struggled and will struggle between aims to advance self inquiry and aims to obstruct it. The aim to obstruct lies not only in the aim to avoid the pains, and pleasures, of facing the music to which self inquiry leads, but in the aim to preserve the pains, and the pleasures, of playing detached and laudable disseminator, or receiver, of arrived "truths."

The most radical, enduring, and worth-conserving contributions — those that most conserve worth and, therefore, are most worth conserving — have come, I believe, and will come from reciprocities of self inquiry. When things go best, psychoanalyst and patient advance their own inquiries and, in the advancing, each other's. This reciprocity asks and creates a fuller mutuality. By a fuller mutuality, I mean not only the mutually satisfying — that alone might only be barter — but a mutual harmony that expresses and favors the beneficial growth of both the patient and the psychoanalyst.

This struggle to advance from the traditional authoritarian to a fuller mutuality has been central to the psychoanalytic encounter from the beginning. It is a struggle that seems to anticipate, reflect, and consolidate the main social thrust of our times.

In the late twentieth century, we begin to look back upon the early twentieth and the nineteenth as a zenith of benign domination, of one-up and one-down, of upstairs and downstairs, in the connections of men to women, parents to children, teachers to students, doctors to patients, politicians to constituents, management to labor, rich to poor, upper classes to lower, nation to nation, race to race, man to nature, and man to things. In the late twentieth, now here and now there, invidious distinctions of status, previously comfortable, begin to sound strange to the ear. Some distinctions, and the related acts of domination, no matter how agreeable in some ways, how useful for some ends, how seemingly "benign" in some intentions, we find increasingly wrong. What, yesterday, seemed "liberal" and "tolerant" today is no longer tolerable. More and more of yesterday's "benign" seems, today, as ruthless as, or more ruthless than, the patently ruthless.

We try, today, if not always more successfully, usually more openly, to overcome inclinations to put down and be put down; we try to honor inclinations to find common ground. These efforts, though not new, and not consistent, seem now more critical; more promising one way, more damaging the other.*

If I were to guess at the unknowable, I would guess that the most pressing needs and the most rewarding opportunities, our new frontiers, now lie in the urgency and the appeal of our search for fuller mutuality. This search, no matter how avidly we pursue it, no more commits us to wild millenarianism than we are committed to unremitting pessimism by Thomas More's "All things will not be well until all men are good, which I do not think will be lo these many long years."

Though the kinds and degrees of mutuality desirable and possible in one place differ from those in another, the struggles in the advancing and the retarding, in the one and the other, seem to me alike enough to encourage me to write of one effort toward a fuller mutuality in the small world of the psychoanalytic ensemble. This is not, therefore, a book on the psychoanalytic method but an inquiry into one aspect that shares common ground with other efforts toward fuller mutuality. And it is not intended as a practical guide to psychoanalysis, or to other efforts, but as a frame within which psychoanalysis, and other efforts, might be considered.

* To call the climate of one's times "critical" may be both cliché and conceit, but it is not, on that score, I think, necessarily wrong.

11

The Analyst's Job

W H E N one of my children was eight or nine, she asked: "What does an analyst do?"

"An analyst," I said, "helps people to decide."

I told of a patient who wondered at work if she should do this first or that, wondered at play if she should play this game or that, wondered at a restaurant if she should eat this food or that.

My daughter listened, looked at me, and asked: "Didn't she wonder if you were the right doctor?"

She did. Soon and often. People are always wondering. They wonder about all sorts of things. They wonder especially who is right for whom.

Today, if I were asked what an analyst does, I would say an analyst helps people to wonder. Circumstances permitting, I'd say an analyst helps people to wonder at center-of-awareness what they've been wondering at edge. An analyst helps — tries to help — people to find what they've been wondering and to pursue it more persistently and respectfully. That is central, I believe, and the rest, implemental.

People are full of wonder. The analyst's job is to help them to find the ways in which they are wonder-ful. People are always inquiring. They inquire into what goes on within and around them. They try to match the one world and the other. They try to unify the fragmentary, the divergent, and the conflicting within themselves and between themselves and others.

At edge-of-awareness, people are always trying to find, to refine, and to make actual their hidden visions of harmony: truth, beauty, goodness, and fairness. They are always trying to make sense of and to make harmonious their feelings, their ideas, their aims, and their acts, one with the other and with those of others.

If people were not trying to do all this, the analyst's job would be as impossible as, or more impossible than, it is said to be. This struggle for unity within self and with others, and the ever-present edge-of-awareness inquiry that quietly seeks it, is what makes humankind most human, and occasionally, kind.

What does it mean to think this way about how we think? Do I weave naive theories of natural rationality, roseate tapestries of innate goodwill? Am I buyer and seller of saccharine? Have I become follower and purveyor of romantic fallacies?

Perhaps so. Some days I feel almost sure.

I have known my share of those who, out of complacency, out of lack of skill, out of fear of what they might find, or out of delight in keeping all in careful disarray, never seem self-inquiring. They seem never to inquire for the advance of mutualities and rarely for any other purpose. I have known those long moments when the voice of self inquiry seemed mute in me and in everyone else I thought I knew.

What can I mean, then, to say we are always inquiring, always seeking now one and now another mutuality? I think what I mean is this:

We all have inclinations and abilities for self inquiry; we all have disinclinations and disabilities. We are always at edge-of-awareness trying to inquire. We are always trying not. We are always trying to advance mutualities and always trying to obstruct. We inquire into aims we try also to hide; we are moved most by aims we try most to hide; we inquire most into aims by which we are most moved. We are always urged to advance and to obstruct; the one urge cannot exist without the other; to underestimate either is a mistake. And it is a mistake easy to make.*

We are always more inquiring than we think, and

---

* It may also be a mistake to suggest a dialectic simpler than the simplest actuality; beyond the urge to inquire and the urge to subvert inquiry, and the urge to advance and to obstruct mutuality, may be the urge to inquire into the tension between the one urge and the other.

always less. We are always more eager and less eager to inquire into, to decide, and to do what we regard best in our natures and in Nature.

Self inquiry is neither the emergency measure of the peculiarly troubled nor the hallmark of a uniquely reflective elite. It is the everyday business of everybody. The most pressing business. We are always for it and against.

The steps of self inquiry may seem large or small, open or hidden. Self inquiry may seem to aim at calling things by their right names, at finding universal truths, or at learning to bake bread. The tone may be lofty or low. Our grasp of what is being inquired into may be full or trivial. But self inquiry is never trivial. It is always about large matters. It always leads to another and another large matter. It always poses questions we can never fully answer and to which we always need, and want, to return.

When I was a student starting out in analysis, a fellow student told of a patient who had put a sign on his desk saying: "People Are Human."

To which our teacher said: "He needs to remind himself."

I think she was right. People are human. We need to remind ourselves. And humans are always trying to inquire into and to advance mutualities. And always trying not. I need to remind myself.

I find it curiously easy to overlook the constancy and the urgency of self inquiry. Or it is not, I suppose, so curious.

Since I see people when their disabilities and disinclinations for self inquiry stand out, and when their motives for defeating self inquiry may be if not stronger, more transparent, and when their hopes rise for an authority who will make self inquiry and its tensions superfluous; and since I struggle with my own needs to play kindly — and unkindly — magician, I fall easily into the mistake of imagining my patients lack the knack of, or even the will for, self inquiry. For all the reasons of my history and of my field for liking one-up and one-down, I take easily to the self-inflating misconception that only through my efforts and example do my patients wish, try, and know self inquiry.

I need to remind myself that each person, patient or not, in special distress or not, with help or not, knowingly or not, and liking it or not, is self-inquiring, whether to bind ill-distinguished tensions, to ease specifiable pains, to define self and other, to renew old pleasures and find new, to assert and to thwart moral claims, to become what he or she wishes he or she were, to build castles in sand and air, to shape interests, theories, and skills. Each struggles to fit one to the other. Each struggles to make noise into music, distraction into picture, and strife into amiable affinities.

I don't know what to call all this. "Wondering" seems too whimsical. "Self inquiry" smacks of dry introspection, misses the point-counterpoint of the awake and the dreamlike, and suggests a solipsistic indifference to what goes on in what we regard as outside our concerns simply because outside our skins.

For want of better words, let's call it self inquiry and say an analyst's job is to help his or her patient to advance his or her ongoing, mostly edge-of-awareness self inquiries. It will do, I think, if we agree we are not talking of *intro*spection, nor of the "life examined" in the Socratic sense, nor of preoccupation with "inner" in the Cartesian sense, but of the full play of experiencing, attention-paying, sense-making, and synthesizing we call self and other. It will do, I think, if we know that even if some of what we refer to seems only about "inner" and some only about "outer," all, whether avowedly about the one or the other, is about both.

We need not take too seriously self inquiry's fleeting bounds. It is always self/other inquiry. We are always making connections and always want to. We cannot think of ourselves without thinking of our surround, nor of our surround without thinking of ourselves. We cannot and we do not want to.

III

Connections

～1

WE ask our patients to tell all. We ask them to tell all they feel, all they think, all they imagine, all they wish, all they fear, all they see, all they hear, all they, in these and other ways, experience. We ask them to tell "whatever comes to mind." "Whatever comes to mind"? A curious phrase. Does it conjure notions of a mind disowned? Never mind. Much must come as visitation before we can call it our own.

Basic tool and basic rule: we ask our patients to tell whatever comes to mind as they lie on the couch trying to tell all. We ask them to feel free to tell all. We ask them to feel obliged to tell all. We don't want to convert inclinations into compulsions. But neither do we want to ignore disinclinations. We want mainly to invite all-telling; we want partly to insist on it. As much as possible the former, no more than necessary the latter.

We ask a daring spontaneity and an unshrinking

honesty; hope for them always, expect them sometimes. We ask our patients to tell all and to attend to all that goes on in the telling. We ask them to attend to the content ordinarily called content, and to the content ordinarily called form, and to all those twists and turns by which content becomes form and form, content. We ask our patients to attend to what comes most alive in the telling. We ask them to attend to their liveliest ways of taking the life out of the telling. We ask them to attend to what they suppose about us, as they tell their stories to us, and to attend to the rise of some suppositions and the fall of others as the story unfolds. We ask for all this in all those unplanned ways passionate interests always assert themselves as invitations.

Our patient writes. But yesterday he could not.

"Damn it," he says, "yesterday I couldn't write *one* word."

(One word: which word, I wonder to myself.)

He tells of effort "*spent*," of time "*lost*," of "*blank*" paper, and of "exercises in *futility*."

He pauses, then says: "The whole day was one long *dry* spell."

(Quaverings of timbre and pitch — I don't know what else — make *dry* stand out. Dry? The word he couldn't write? Dry. Desert. Thirsty. Lost Patrol. Oasis. Mirage. Dry spell?)

"What else comes to mind," I ask, "about a *dry* spell?"

"I couldn't write one word," he says.

(I hear his warning; he means to go ahead, and not. I wonder if he has noticed he has come full circle. A little "dry spell" now perhaps? I wonder whether to ask. I choose not. I cannot choose otherwise; he has gone ahead.)

He tells of a poem he had wanted, but been unable, to write. He doesn't tell much.

"I can't tell poems in the making," he says. "If I do, my muse *dries* up."

"The poem," he says, "is about walking alone on the outer beach."

(*Alone* and *outer*. He makes them sound very alone and very outer. Alones and outers, dry spells, outer reaches, and outer beaches. I see a shore I once knew. Short stretch of quiet river. Flat brown barge that *crawls* to Yonkers.)

"Writing in my room is *so hard*," he says. "I wonder why I can't write. . . . Maybe because it's so *cold* and *dark*."

He stops. He bends his knees way up. He crosses his arms, pulls them tight to his chest, digs his head into the couch.

(Is he cold?)

For a few minutes he lies still. Silent. Motionless.

(I think of his cold and dark room, then of another, then of a room I lived in once when I went off to school. An attic room.)

He looks out the window. He lifts his head as if to leave. He settles back, and then goes on.

He tells of a room with large windows and a north light, then of another with morning sun, then one he lived in with *"great"* roommates, a *"wonderful"* room, a *"great"* room. He remembers a room in a *"grand"* hotel, and another, another, and then a room in his childhood home, a *"living* room, with a *big* fireplace to cook in," he says, "and a couch to sleep on and a *great* goose-down *comforter* my *grand*mother made."

(Why so many greats and grands, I wonder silently. To "comfort"? Against "too dark" and "too cold"?)

I say: "Those were warmer and brighter rooms than you live in now."

"Much," he says.

(I think I hear him swallow.)

He pauses a few seconds — they seem longer — and says: "Maybe remembering them makes me feel better."

He pauses again. Then he thinks of shopping he "must" do later. He thinks of books he will buy for his nephew for Christmas, of how pleased the boy will be, of how pleased he himself had been with the books his father had given, books piled high under the tree at Christmas in the *living* room.

(Books piled high, books now hard to write. A brother has died. A room is too cold and too dark. Alone. Outer. Lost. Dry. Who walks alone on which outer beach? My thoughts are going one way; his have gone another.)

He imagines now a *"great"* shopping spree: one store, then another, one gift and another, one recipient delighted and another. He laughs and says: "I love to play Santa."

(Where have all the dry spells gone?) I say: "Maybe thinking of playing Santa helps you to feel better."

He says: "Yes, I didn't notice. I think I do that when I feel sad. I go shopping. I buy things. I buy for myself or for others. I mean I really buy them, or, I do it in my head. Then, I don't feel sad."

"You don't?"

"Well, not as sad," he says. "Well, I feel sad but I don't notice."

The hour is over. There will be other hours, and more of the sadness he doesn't notice.

~ 2

A RUN of associations, even brief as this, can be seen many ways, put to many purposes. Most analysts, however, of whatever predilection or persuasion, would begin, I believe, by trying to gain a sense of how "everything flows." They would look for a composition, a unity — form leading to flux, and flux to form — shaped by the associator's emerging urges and emotions.

It is Christmas. Alone in his room, his cold and dark room, alone in his writing and most on his own, our patient yearns most to be protected, directed, and comforted. Among those he misses most — and is pleased to have missing — is an older brother who died years ago, shortly before Christmas.

Long receiver of books and of other revered and resented hand-me-downs, our patient is now book-buyer, book-giver, and off and on book-writer. Long struggler to walk alone, long walker in brother's and others' footsteps, he struggles now to write his poem of the rewards and costs of walking alone. Some days he cannot or will not take the "first" step.

In earlier hours, he has told of others (not he) who are alone: first, long ago and far away, and then, now and close by. In this hour, he tells straight out of himself, alone at Christmas, alone in his writing, alone in his cold and dark room, and alone on the outer beach.* Now he faces, almost faces, the sadness he feels — and the ways he manages not to feel — when he is, or imagines being, alone.

---

* Soon, he will tell, too, of feeling alone in his analysis: "You don't help me as much as you used to." "You don't give me enough food for thought."

Re-consider. The voyage of the couch begins in the cold and dark room where he lives and cannot write, then moves to the outer beach where he walks alone, then moves back to his room, then to the window of the analytic room, then to brighter and brighter rooms, to the "wonderful" room, the "great" room with "great" roommates (now no longer alone), to a "grand" hotel, and at last, to a "living" room in his childhood home, a room with a "big" fireplace to "cook" in, a couch to "sleep" on, and a "great" goose-down "comforter" "grand"mother made. He is carried, and we are carried, from the challenges and failures of writing to visions of being taken care of, of shopping, and of playing Santa, from lonely discomforts to creature comforts, from the emptiness of today to the fullness of yesterday, from the sadness felt, or almost felt, in the analytic hour, to the joys of childhood, and from the analytic couch on which he now lies to the couch of long ago on which he was warmed, fed, comforted, and could sleep.*

The analyst of one school will have a sharper eye, ear, or whatever for some matters than the analyst of another, and any will differ from another, but all, I assume, are concerned as I was then, and as we have been now, with discerning connections. Though we cannot always pay

---

* We are talking, of course, of today's versions of yesterday's pleasures; our business is not History, but history as it has been by him, for the moment, writ.

attention to connections — at least, not self-consciously — when we proceed at our best, we proceed, I believe, with a peripheral vision, or an effort toward a peripheral vision, of ties between what we focus on and the larger composition of which it seems part. (The more we see connections, the more we see character.) Conversely, doing what we do at our worst, we proceed with a minor regard, or a major indifference, for connections.

Unfortunately, however, our language for considering these matters is a Pidgin English of isolated words and phrases that make a useful sense for some purposes, but are as unsuited for describing continuities as it would be to call the shimmering and shifting light of twilight gray. More unfortunately, the constrictions of our language impose constrictions on our vision.

Even proceeding with whatever respect we can manage for how one thing connects with another, we shall not always be sure how things connect, why they connect, and how those connections — we call them "free associations" — advance self inquiry.

Looking one way, I see a patient belabored. I see feelings emerging, associations arising, alien forces pressing for expression, and alien forces blocking the way. I see hidden urges and pains, and hidden ways to satisfy those urges and ease those pains. I see loneliness and longings to be fed, warmed, and swaddled. I see all these escaping from earlier containment through a laudable loosening brought on by analysis: couch, supine position, invisible hearer, the right and requirement to tell all, and the occasional relevance of my occasional remarks. Looking so, though I count on my patient to tell all, I regard what he tells — at least that which I prize most — as emerging, coming up, and connecting one thing and another, mainly despite himself.

Seen so, the associative flow has, so to speak, a life of its own. And putting matters so, I highlight his inability or unwillingness to inquire into events taking place within but somehow without him. I highlight, too, my own efforts to inquire into what I regard useful to inquire into but he, largely, does not.

From this angle of vision I see quite a lot. I see his associations driven by urges and feelings provoked from within and by the events of Christmas, of writing, and of analysis. I see Christmas reminding him of what he once had but now does not (and now has but once did not), writing asking him to be alone both physically and in seeing and saying things his own way — "This is the first poem," the poet says and each time must dare to say — and analysis asking him to tell his tale with fewer interruptions and interferences than he has been accustomed to arrange. Feeling, therefore, more alone and freer to feel it, he wants more to be cared for, and wanting more to be cared for, he feels more alone. From barren to fertile loneliness, he has a way to go.*

And looking so, I see him take off in flight from these urges and feelings to fancies of soothings and comfortings of warmer and brighter rooms, of shopping, locomotion, jocularity, Santaism, and more. All this then becomes "grist for the mill" of inquiry. My inquiry, that is. And whatever of that inquiry my patient reluctantly joins.

⁓ 3

THAT on the one hand, this on the other:

To say we are all, more than we know, blind robots, all pushed by forces of which we are — and try to be — unaware, is to say quite a lot. If I try to say more, I don't want to say less.

But neither do I want to see my patient, and therefore myself, as *nothing* but blind robot. I want to know the ways we are both blind robots and not, both driven

---

* Things being complex enough already, I omit the memories, phantasies, and other reruns of toddlerdom — turns from mother to brother, from talking to walking, and from walking to talking — to which we were later led.

and driving. If one aim of analytic inquiry is to face the raw urges and feelings, counter-urges and counter-feelings, that drive our associations and us, surely our contrapuntal concern is with those organized and organizing interests and inquiries that join old brain and new.

Our patient asks why he cannot write; he wonders if he cannot because his room is so cold and dark. Taken one way, his question is barely a question: more a cry of frustration. Taken another way, his question, and his answer, is an open inquiry into all for which *writing* and *rooms* stand. After all, we are not talking of real estate, but of one space and another, inner and outer, one image and another, one urge and another, one feeling and another, of all his private, semiprivate, and public "rooms."

Taken one way, his answer lays all his troubles on his cold and dark room, and puts an end to inquiry. Taken another, his answer is just right: when he tries to write, his room is surely too cold and too dark.

Taken the second way, his question and reply open inquiry into all that he means by *write*, by *room*, by *too cold*, and *too dark*. *Write* as in "one word"? To whom? For what? *Room* as in where he "lives"? Today's room? Yesterday's? The consulting room? *Cold* as in cold and lonely? *Cold* as in cold feet? *Dark* as in dark and gloomy? *Dark* as in dark and scary?

Or is it only we who know that "everything is
metaphor"? I believe not. I want to remember our
patient knows too, knows and means to find what in
some "room" he already knows: the meanings of his
metaphors, the petrified and the lively. I want to know
that when he goes from the cold and dark room where
he "couldn't write one word" to the rooms warmer and
brighter, he may not only be trying to avoid today's
pains by imagining yesterday's pleasures, but reminding
himself of all he misses, and inquiring, therefore, or
almost inquiring, into the pains he is also trying to avoid.

I think he is trying to proceed both more construc-
tively and more obstructively than he or I know. I
think that when he shifts from thoughts of "being alone
and unable to write" to thoughts of "walking, shopping,
giving books, and playing Santa," he is not only fleeing
the painful, but replaying and inquiring into the very
flights he arranges in fact or in fancy when in his cold
and dark room he tries and is unable to write. I think
that in shifting from one image to another he is not
only fleeing; he is recreating and exploring, as he lies
quietly on the couch rushing about, all those rooms of
the mind in which it is not simply a matter of cold or of
warm, of dark or of light, of having Santa or of playing
Santa, but of all on a spectrum where cold/warm, dark/
light, having Santa/being Santa are all of a piece, and
advance and retreat are not sharply distinct, and every-

thing, like *Ciao*, means hello *and* goodbye. Where opposite becomes apposite, we know, and our patient knows, the chances for inquiry are most promising.

Inquiry leads to inquiry leads to inquiry. In one hour he is concerned with the "solitary confinement" of a prisoner; in another, with the "peaceful" meditations of a Trappist monk (silent of course); in another, with Lindbergh's flight and his book *We*; and finally, in this hour, with his "cold and dark" room and the writing of his own solo: "walking alone on the outer beach." He moves our inquiry from solitudes forced to solitudes chosen, from stunned outcast to inquiring holy man, from criminal to explorer-writer, from solitudes of lying low to those of flying high, from solitudes of barely endurable emptiness and terror to those of imagined "we"-ness, from helplessness to brave action blended with bookishness, and from unnameable pains to the pains and pleasures of his flights of imagination, his writing, and other "first steps."*

The sentences of his inquiry are one of a kind; the words and the syllables, I believe, are not. He inquires over and over — and who does not? — into the challenges of solitude and into the threats of isolation. He inquires into mutualities of fence-building and into mutualities of leave-taking. He inquires into ways to let

---

* "Walking alone" and "first steps" led soon to a sense of "walking ahead" of the analyst, and much later, to "walking without" him.

go but to keep in touch, ways to look ahead but to look back, ways to walk away but to find a way home.

Borders between juxtaposition for exploration and juxtaposition for evasion are shadowy. No. There are no borders. Exploration and evasion fill the same room.

We are all always both clarifying and obfuscating. I don't want to underestimate him, her, and me by thinking he, she, and I are doing only one or the other. The connections of content to form, particularly when free association is most free, are persistently shaped and reshaped so that juxtapositions, reversals, ambiguities, and other spectral qualities both expose and hide, advance and delay the ongoing edge-of-awareness inquiries the free associator is almost but not quite ready to acknowledge.

The suspicious analyst will see the delay of inquiry; the sanguine analyst, the advance. Ideally, we move easily from the one view to the other. But it's a long way to heaven; and in analysis as elsewhere it is mainly a matter of meanwhiles. Meanwhile, we struggle to steer between the suspicious and the sanguine and to avoid a fixed course between.

Looking one way, I see mechanical forces pressing for expression and mechanical forces pressing for suppression. Looking the other, I see my patient searching for the conflicts for which his budding solutions are almost but not quite ready. Looking one way, I see free association producing pop-ups for inquiry. Looking another, since those pop-ups had been shaped in the first place by the free associator's edge-of-awareness inquiries, they help me to find and to help the free associator to find what the free associator was right along trying, and trying not, to inquire into.

When things go best, I look both ways at once; I see that when my patient and I "free associate," we are always trying to discover, and not, what at edge-of-awareness we were already trying to discover, and not: a name forgot, a small link, and a whole new universe. Inquiry advances, intentionally and not; inquiry seems to break down, intentionally and not; inquiry seeming to break down leads, intentionally and not, to new inquiry. Form becomes flux becomes form becomes flux. Seeing double we see most clearly.

When things go best, my patient and I do not search for new things to explore. We search for what is already being explored, explored and avoided. Search? Or let it dawn? Both. We both do both, sometimes more one, sometimes more the other, but always both, alternately and together. Both connect, disconnect, and reconnect one thing and another: things thought, seen, felt, smelled, heard, and otherwise perceived, each separately, and with the other.

IV

Duet

ONCE, hiking on a high mountain trail, some friends and I came upon a woman in distress. Waving to us frantically and pointing to a spot in the grass, she screamed: "A snake! A snake! I hate snakes!"

Oddly, though, for each step she retreated she took at least a step forward. Some steps forward being longer than some backward, she was advancing slowly toward the spot at which she pointed and the snake she said she hated.

Later, seated with my wife by the side of a lake, I was musing about this incident when two canoeists paddled by. One of the canoeists, in response to my wife's comment about the beauty of the scene and of their canoe, smiled and said: "I deserve it."

It occurred to me that to both snake-hater and deserving canoeist, one might, if prepared to face the consequences, have replied correctly, though neither tactfully nor helpfully: "You are wondering."

If it is true the woman was wondering whether she hated snakes, and the canoeist whether he was deserving, how do we know it? We don't. We suspect it. But why?

We might say that every statement is the answer to a question and often more than one answer to more than one question. If I say: "Look at that beautiful maple," I seem to ask and to answer: "What is that? A tree."

"What kind? A maple."

"How does it look? Beautiful."

And I may also be asking and answering what should and shouldn't be looked at, and what should and shouldn't be judged beautiful, and wondering and asking if you share my view.

In the case of the woman who said she hated snakes, we might suspect she is in doubt about her snake hatred not only because we believe all statements contain questions but because of what we take to be the peculiar force of her assertion of the obvious, and, even more, the glaring discrepancy between her words and acts. We might go so far as to suspect she is asking a question to which words and acts pose alternative answers. In the case of the canoeist, we might infer a question about deservedness on the grounds of the gratuitous nature of his remark and the contrast between what he said and what we expect in small talk between strangers in such circumstances.

But such explanations of how we spot lurking questions — let alone which — are unconvincing. Nor is it more convincing if we say that in each instance the speaker raised a question in our minds: "If you hate snakes, why are you going toward one?" and "Why do you raise the matter of whether you deserve it?"

From our questions, we may have inferred muffled questions in the speaker, but we may have inferred incorrectly. *We* have the questions; the speaker may or may not.

And even if there is a rough fit between the speakers' questions and our own, we cannot be sure whether the snake-hater is narrowly pursuing questions about snakes or raising larger questions about what she hates and does not, what she loves and does not, what to approach and what not; nor can we know if our deserving canoeist is narrowly concerned with one thing he deserves or not, whether he is a great moralist, carries a crippling burden of scrupulosity, or is sharing a private joke about the ethics, or failure of ethics, of modern advertising. We can only be sure that we all ask a lot of questions; looked at one way they are silly, another way, grand.

But suppose in some ways I cannot fully grasp I am able sometimes to "resonate" to the other's questions, to "put myself in his or her place," to "intuit," "perceive," or otherwise fathom the questions almost but not quite asked. If I am prepared to "see" questions on such evidence as this — evidence as in evidently, not evidence as in proof — I might see questions all over the place. I do. I see questions not only in statements, but in dress, in dreams, in symptoms, in gestures, in possessions, in intentions, in inventions, and even in questions.

Since I have come to believe that my job is to help my patients to advance their questions (questions almost but not quite asked, shackled questions waiting to be let out), I have been trying to understand what guides my choice among all the questions my patients may be — seem to be — pursuing. Clearly I do not regard it as my job to pursue any and all questions. What, then, am I looking for?

It's hard to say. In general, I seem to be looking for questions that are pressing and tolerable. Or almost tolerable. Free association seems to help my patient and me to find questions that are strong, repetitive, and ready, or almost ready, to be advanced from the corner of the eye to the center. That does narrow the range a bit.

But even if I could specify more clearly which questions I am seeking, would that answer the question of which questions I finally settle on? If I regard myself as seeking, and sometimes finding, questions almost but not quite asked (whatever the content may be), do I imagine things taking place simply "in" my patient and imagine myself simply observing, and responding to, what is "there"? If I "put myself" in my patient's place, which self do I put and in which of my patient's places?

Is nothing, then, in the eye, and ear, of the beholder? Am I a camera? Does a camera record only what is "there"? Am I a tabula rasa on which my patient writes?

I have told myself that the myth of plain seeing is a useful myth and to let it alone. But the question comes back. If I regard myself as "pure" observer, am I a believer, then, in "doctrines of immaculate perception"?

I seem to be. But the telling question, I think, is not whether I am a believer, but whether an unreformable one.

In the first moments of finding what my patient is inquiring into, I seem to be convinced that what I perceive is clearly and only what is "there." In these moments I forget — I think I must — what I know, or have heard, of the effect of the observer on the observed. Or the observed on the observer. I trust my findings fully; otherwise I split hairs. In the theatre of fact, as much as of fiction, I must put belief at center-of-awareness and disbelief at edge. Only in a second or subsequent look do I seem able to look critically at how I look, and even then I can only occasionally discover what I know well enough in the abstract but not so well in its intimate particulars:

When I find whatever I find, I find what I am looking for. I must have an idea what I am looking for, and a need to find it.

I recall a time when this fact was brought particularly sharply to my attention, outside the consultation room. I had gone to a meeting in one of those inns whose anglophile ambience pushes an eighteenth-century gentility. As I walked through a room on the way to the room where the meeting was to occur, I glanced at a long wall. At one end was a panel with a picture of a squire, and at the other, a panel with a picture of a woman of the same class and era, presumably the squire's "lady." Without giving it much thought, I noticed only the labored arrangement, maudlin content, sexist overtones, and the consistency of the pictures and other things in, and going on in, the inn.

Several hours later, the meeting over, I retraced my steps. I again saw the wall with the panels with the pictures. But now I saw at once what I had failed to see before. What earlier were panels were not panels but doors. And the trivial pictures were not trivial at all; they marked the doors to the "Men's Room" and the "Ladies' Room."

We find what we are looking for. Of course. All we perceive, all we register, all we recall, all we think, all we imagine, all we feel, all we do, is shaped by what we are looking for.

When I find what my patient is inquiring into, I find what I am looking for. What I am looking for depends not only on what my patient now says and has earlier

44

said, and on what I earlier selected and collected and
now reselect and re-collect, and on all my earlier and
present experiences professional and non-, and on all
my preferences, hunches, and theories of disorder, treat-
ment, and cure, but on all the urges, feelings, moods,
phantasies, and all else of body and mind that mold my
sensitivities and my insensitivities.

And all this is shaped by and shapes what I am, at
edge-of-awareness, inquiring into. What I find, then,
when I find what my patient is inquiring into, is what
I am inquiring into. When I find my patient's ongoing
edge-of-awareness questions, I find my own.*

We are always asking questions. Our questions are
always in search of other questions, and of the questions of others. We are all of a kind. We are one of a
kind. If the risk is that what I see over there is not both
here and there but more here than there, taking that risk
is the best I can do. And it is best I do it.

To match two inquiries, I must not look too fixedly
or I shall be looking for the identical rather than the
similar. The similar is all it is possible to find; flexible
inquiry and monomania are not the same. I must be
able to inquire, to drop the inquiry, and to return to it,
over and over, so that by seeing something in different

---

* I want to mention this now and come back to it later: my edge-of-
awareness inquiries are for myself at least as much as for my
patient.

moods, I may be able to see it more clearly and see better what is match and what is mismatch.

When things go well, my patient's self inquiry meets mine in complex and seamless connection. And having found a good fit between my patient's self inquiry and my own, I may say I have been objective. But I can only mean — and I should be pleased to mean — I have been objective in matching subjectivities.

V

On Seeing Things

~ 1

TEN or so years ago I decided to take a fresh look at how an analyst listens. I decided, that is, to take a fresh look at how one analyst listens. But what was a fresh look? "Unconscious to unconscious," "negative capability," "willing suspension of disbelief": what do we do when we do what we do and how can we possibly "see" it?

Having tried half-dozen or more ways to look at how I listened, and having found that in the looking I was disrupting most what I wanted most not to disrupt, I settled at last upon a way of looking, after the fact. As soon after hours as I could, usually while my patient and I were parting, I tried to let my mind run quickly over the events of the hour till I came upon one or two most vivid.

Although some patients remarked on my peculiar

faraway expression — thereby distinguishing it from other peculiar faraway expressions of which I am capable — neither their reactions to me nor my reactions to their reactions posed unmanageable problems for them or for me. But I found I was not forming the lively and compact impressions for which I had hoped. Instead I was belaboring detailed and dreary reports of the particulars. For the purposes at hand, the habits and rituals of organized case reporting were too much upon me, and with them the incompetence that comes of too many years of recording events in ways useful (if and when useful) for other purposes.

I needed practice to escape my practice. I needed practice to allow my thoughts to range more freely: to allow or to induce those drifts after the hour that I more commonly allow or induce during the hour and whenever else the call of organization is not too strong. When finally I managed such drifts, I found the impressions I was seeking. That is, I found something. I found myself, over and over, trying to find words for visual images.

Looking this way, I have become aware of thousands of images. I have set down hundreds in words, and, along with them, immediate associations, associations at the end of the day, and associations weeks, months, and sometimes years later. Here is an instance, the first in which the workings became, with the image, visible:

One day, on rising to show my patient out, I saw in

my mind's eye a small black dog sitting in and looking out through a tall arched doorway, the center entrance of a large white house. I realized that early in the hour, when my patient had told of visiting friends "to help to build a dog-house," I had seen this same image. I realized, too, that on the first seeing, I had taken this to be an illustration of something my patient had said, an illustration without modification, and I had paid it no particular attention. Now, however, after the hour, I felt sure that what I had seen earlier was what I had again seen now, not a dog in a dog-house at all, but a dog in a two-story white Colonial, large enough to be a house for humans. I had seen, that is, a dog in a man-house.

I then recalled what had followed my patient's mention of the dog-house and my seeing the dog in the man-house. A half hour or more in the original, and choppy, it was now in the rerun a few seconds and all of a piece: my patient telling details of a visit to the friends he had helped to build the dog-house, and then of another friend, and another, and another, and I, except for asking a question here and there, listening in silence, puzzling, failing to make more than surface sense, wrestling with questions whether he was not yet where he was going, whether he was there but I not, whether I had wax in my third ear, wrestling, that is, with all those familiar tensions of noncomprehension that I know to be, and more or less convincingly assure myself to be, the expectable darkness before the dawn. Expectable or not, it is always unsettling. Finally, my patient, as if grasping what he had been trying to say all along and now wanting to put things simply and straight, said: "You know, whenever I visit friends, no matter how well I know them, and how much I like them and they like me, I have to do something for them. I have to bring a story, do some work, give a gift. I have to have a ticket of admission."

All this came back quickly in my after-the-hour drift, and on that border between recall and relive, I again saw my dog in the man-house. I recalled that when my patient had said he needed a "ticket of admission," I had said: "You seem to feel you are in the dog-house and need to do something special to get into the main house."

Having said it, I had become aware that we were talking of many things, including how my patient had been acting with me. And, having meant simply to resay what he had said and to join it with the language he had used — if one can say simply what one means at such moments — I was unprepared for the rush and the range of his reply.

One thought tumbling out after another as if he had too much to say and too few words or too little time to say it, he replied that this was the story of his life; that though he always had food and shelter, he always "needed permission to be admitted to the company of people"; that he was like his family's dogs who lived outside, who always had food and shelter but rarely were allowed in the house, and then only if "quiet, subdued, and clean"; that he always wondered whether what the dogs went through was "worth it," and whether, rather than being "regimented and sanitized," they were better off "outside, free, smelling natural smells, rolling around in their own shit, and doing whatever they liked by themselves." All this he said with such concern he seemed to be one of the dogs and to speak for them and himself.

As I thought of all this — still in those minutes after the hour — thought about what he had said and I had said, and about the dog in the man-house, I recalled that when my patient had first said he visited friends *to* help them to build a dog-house, rather than visited *and* helped them to build a dog-house, I had felt puzzled. I had felt puzzled by his priorities and the sureness with which he announced those priorities: It was then I first *saw* my dog in the man-house.

A piece of the puzzle seemed to fit. His remark about the dog-house, and its implied priorities of service and friendship, must have reminded me of something I knew all along, or almost knew; must have met and rounded out an impression of him that I had already formed, but not fully grasped: that he tended to feel

53

unwelcome and to justify and buy friendship by stressing services performed or performable. At edge-of-awareness I seemed to have told in visual image what I could not yet tell myself in words: he was like a dog who must do tricks to be admitted to a man-house. When he later spoke of needing a "ticket of admission," I, informed by his words and by my image, had been able to say: "You seem to feel you are in the dog-house and need to do something special to get into the main house." (Dog-house, man-house, main house — how oddly these images slide.)

Having made this beginning toward re-viewing my dog in the man-house, and toward seeing something of how I had used him, I found myself annoyed. I was annoyed that putting the image into words seemed to lose so much in the translation. I was annoyed that I had to work so hard to recover the image and to make such small sense of it. The whole matter struck me as not worth pursuing. And although at another time I might have found my sudden annoyance interesting, at this time I did not. I was unaware that my annoyance was a piece of the earlier events I was re-viewing. I felt inclined to drop the inquiry; since other matters now called for my attention, I had no trouble finding good reason to indulge the inclination.

That evening, however, I felt a renewed interest in

the dog in the man-house. Fortified by that silent after-work, and whatever else makes us more ready to approach what before we would not — and without which self inquiry would be even slower and more limited than it is — I resumed what I had begun. Determined to make up for the short shrift I had given it earlier, I re-viewed my image, and, approaching it as we might the analysis of a dream, I began by associating to its elements.

The dog. He has a dog. They live together. They romp together like two persons. Like John and Henry. Henry has a dog. He talks to the dog as if to a person. A talking dog? A listening dog. RCA logo: his master's voice.

Putting on the dog. Putting on airs. Looking fancy. Looking fancy for the analysis. He cleans up his language. Talks jargon. Leaves things out. Leaves the dog out. The dog out back.

A dog does tricks. He does tricks. He does what he thinks I want to hear. The entertainer. Brings a gift. Apple for the teacher. A ticket of admission? A diller, a dollar, a ten o'clock scholar. He comes at ten. When he comes.

Dog in a house. This house. Dog on the analytic couch. Locked up. Locked out. One day some children rang the bell to find out why a poor dog was locked in a car. Dog in a car. Dog in a man-house. A separate house. A house out back. Alone. A room.

A room apart. Dog in a man-house. Man in a dog-house.

Dog in a courthouse. Lord Jim. On trial. "That dirty dog." A sea dog. A sea dog who failed in his duty. Messes up. In the dog-house.

(I was aware that I was visualizing a scene from the admiralty trial in Conrad's Lord Jim, the scene in which Jim hears someone call him a "dirty dog," wheels and sees that a man behind him had made innocent reference to a real dog.)

Little dog. Little dog in a big house. Little boy in a big room. Big rooms and big houses. A lofty house with a big door. His house. My father's house. My father's house has many mansions.

A big door. An arch. The door to a dog-house. Door to a cathedral. Arched. Vaulted. High door. High house. High hat. The roof points up. Aspires. A spire. American Gothic. All work and no play. Dog in a man-house. House dog. Cocker spaniel. Cocky. He runs in and out as he pleases. Lord of the manor. A man's house is his castle. Or does this dog own this house?

(The image of a dog now shifted to an image of a small boy. I was reminded of an old photograph from a family album and then of my family's album and of a photograph I had seen years ago of me at six or seven alone on the high limb of a tree.)

Out on a limb. A hiding place. Tom Sawyer. Huck Finn. A raft. A hut. We built a hut. He built a house. A house apart. Two little houses apart with high doors. Sanctuary in a city lot. Kids running. Dogs in the park No more pencils, no more books, no more teacher's dirty looks.

(I saw a parallel now in the work of my patient's father and my father, and in the particular mix of respect and rebellion with which in adolescence we had greeted them, our fathers, who were in a sense teachers and preachers though literally neither.)

Our fathers. Our fathers who art in heaven? Teachers and preachers. Churches and cathedrals. Europe. Rome. The steps of St. Paul. No, St. Peter.

(Here, the flow of my associations stopped. Or rather, it shifted. I began to wonder why I had made the mistake of substituting St. Paul for St. Peter.)

Paul in the place of Peter? Robbing Peter to pay Paul?

I thought then of the summer of my thirteenth year when travelling with my family and having been taken to see one great cathedral after another, and having been instructed by my father in their considerable glories, I sat down on the steps of St. Peter's and asserted my unwillingness to enter yet another. I recalled with a touch of my original glee my father's dismay when, in that much overused and what I knew to be overloaded expression, I said: "If you've seen one, you've seen them all."

I thought then of strikes, sit down and stand up, and of Luther, and suddenly, still picturing and savoring my moment of defiance, I realized that my position in the arched doorway of the great cathedral, as I now imagined it, was the same as that of my dog in the arched doorway of the man-house.

～ 2

If I try now to be analyst to myself and to my patient, I shall try not to dive into the depths where both would be over our heads. And I shall try not to get too far ahead of us, which is to say, not to get too far behind.

Whenever and wherever I approach the dog in the man-house, I find the same thing. I find he is two-faced. I find my patient; I find myself.

Whenever and wherever I look, I find allusions to ways my patient and I are alike. I find allusions to likenesses of experience. I find allusions to likenesses of character. I find allusions to likenesses past and to likenesses present. Each detail of my dog in the man-house, pushed far enough, proves biography and autobiography.

The "white house" leads by more than one route to old aspirations, of my patient's and mine (aspirations, if not papal or presidential, "high"). The "white house" leads to old "dog-houses" in which we hunkered in shame, stood in defiance, and struggled to live more on the level. The "white house" leads to a house in which my patient lived as a boy and to another in which I lived as a boy, houses haunted, enlarged, and enlivened by similar yearnings and fears. The "white house" leads to houses past in which he and I had faced and failed to face strivings we were facing and failing to face in the hour of the dog in the man-house.

The dog, emblem of those struggles, spoke over and over of dogs my patient remembered from his childhood and dogs I would not have thought I remembered, but did, from my childhood. And so it went with each detail of the image and of my associations to it.

Lord Jim spoke of gaps between my patient's acts and ideals, between his father's acts and ideals, between my acts and ideals, and between my father's acts and ideals. *Lord Jim* spoke of nautical settings in my patient's life and mine that wove these allusions together. *Lord Jim* spoke of self-critical propensities and ways of warding them off. My patient's and his father's, mine and my father's. An apple for the teacher, Huck Finn, a hut on a vacant lot, a sit-down strike, each led in more than one way to my patient and to me in like circumstances of self and surround.

The dog in the man-house does not tell *the* story of my patient's life, nor does it tell *the* story of mine. It tells *a* story for both over a long period of time, but especially at that time. When I first saw the dog in the man-house I was aware of part of that story. Part I have become aware of since. Part, you have seen and will see, I cannot yet bear to see.

Struggles of sons with fathers and fathers with sons, long shadows of earlier struggles and earlier "lessons," hostilities couched in kindness and kindness in hostilities, blurred boundaries between the one and the other, no-saying to define one from the other, grandiose and grand, candor and sham. Consider a piece:

You may have guessed — you will understand if I tell — my father was a culture-hound. An aspiring culture-hound. He was master, and therefore captive, of academic "putting on the dog." Social strivings for "high" class, lofty humility of the scholar, agony and ecstasy of underdog with overview, elitist voice for hoi polloi, all these blended with all his talents and all his limits. *Tel pere, tel fils?** You will judge gently my fierce tug-of-war between imitation and rebellion.

* *Tel pere, tel fils?* What kind of way is that to talk? My father's.

I was angry at my father for reasonable reasons and for unreasonable. He was angry at me for reasonable reasons and for unreasonable. Each was angry, that is, for reasons we might now call reasonable and for reasons from other realms of reason.

Let me speak for myself and, I hope, also for him I was angry at my father for "dragging" me to see what I regarded to be, and for reasons I regarded to be, sham. "This must be Belgium. It is Tuesday." Or is it, "This must be Tuesday. It is Belgium"? I was angry and I was confused. I could not see the border between my father's seeking of dubious distinctions and his intentions to help me to see what he really thought, and I suspected, to be worth seeing. I was angry that he was pretending to be what he was not, which was not as good as he was. And I was especially angry that he was stopping me from seeing what I most wanted to see. Most wanted? Well, surely as much as old cathedrals. You will have seen from my fractious remark on the steps of St. Peter's ("If you've seen one, you've seen them all"), and from my preoccupations with show and tell, and look and see, and showing and telling by looking and seeing, the conflicting agendas upon which I felt my father to intrude. The only trace I was aware of then — at least the only trace I can retrace now — was my idea that by taking me to see all these sights, my father was preventing me from going to the spicy sex shows of which my companions at home had told me. I was particularly indignant because I secretly suspected that this high-level sight-seeing was a piece of hypocrisy designed to hide and to bar me from the low-level stuff I was sure my father, and probably my mother, went to after I had been bedded down for the night.*

When I first saw my dog in the man-house, my patient and I, more than either knew, were reliving and reconsidering old views in which demeaned and feared feelings and urges were seen to be animal and alien and to require decoration and locking up in our persons, which in turn were seen to be animal, alien, and locked up in our circumstances. Dogs in man-houses and men in dog-houses.

My patient was locking up anger. He was angry at me for "forcing" him to come to analysis. That is, he was almost but not quite aware of being angry at me for what he found wrong with my "guidance." Just as I, when I sat down on the steps of St. Peter's, had been almost but not quite aware of being angry at my father for what I had found wrong with his.

And *I* was locking up anger. I was angry at my patient for judging me petty tyrant, for judging me in

---

* My distress was only slightly tempered by nightly readings of De Kruif's *Microbe Hunters*, a copy of which I'd brought on the trip, and in which I had found the most interesting hunter to be Van Leeuwenhoek, inventor of and looker into the microscope.

a way I judged to be unfair. And for judging me in a way I judged to be fair. I was angry at him, too, for thinking so little of himself and of me that he found it necessary to produce, for the petty tyrant, tickets of admission. I was almost but not quite aware of being angry.

Each was indignant. Each was hiding the indignation in forced "helpfulness." But each feared and hid his anger less than before. Each was struggling to face indignations and to find boundaries between the proper and the preposterous. Each was trying to break shackles of false gentility and those other self-selected, borrowed, and imposed restraints to which Thoreau referred, I think, when he said: "What demon could have possessed me that I behaved so well?"

In the hour of the dog in the man-house, my patient's telling me of the building of a dog-house, my seeing of the dog in the man-house, my saying: "You seem to feel in the dog-house and you need to do something special to get into the main house," and my patient's remembering the "dogs out back," were the first steps — perhaps first visible steps — in each becoming more aware of the struggles in which we were involved. The tensions pre-viewed in the dog in the man-house soon came more into the open.

On the day after the appearance of the dog in the man-house, and the talk of tickets of admission and the "dogs out back," my patient said he felt "sick to [his] stomach." "It's a good feeling," he added. "And it would be nice to throw up. It would be nice to throw up all over the place."

"Better than being sanitized," I replied, referring, of course, to his thought of the previous hour.

"Yes," he said, "letting loose." He thought then of times he had feared going places, feared throwing up in public, wetting the bed, soiling, expressing himself, committing himself, making a fool of himself, being pigeonholed, being made to feel small and a nuisance. In following hours, he felt "cooped up" in his analysis, "forced to come prepared with a story," "pissed off" at me, "squeezing out feelings (rage) in small spasms," and wanting to "throw" them with "force."

Months later, more at home with himself, with his feelings, with his impulses, with his present, with his past, and with me, and less inclined to play "faithful" inferior (Fido?), he dreamed he took a dog whom he "ordinarily would have left out" into "a high-ceilinged room" in which he had talked often with his father, which reminded him, by contrast, of the low-ceilinged room in which he talked often with me. He was surprised, he said, that in the dream he felt so comfortable, and, despite being with his dog, so acceptable.

You will have some notion of what changes had taken place — and not — in my patient, and in me, between the moment of the dog in the man-house and this dream. Probably you don't find it strange that an image formed by one person in the presence of another — my dog in the man-house in the presence of my patient — should contain more of what the image-maker knows, or thinks he knows, of self and of other, than the image-maker knows he knows, or thinks he knows. Probably, therefore, you don't find it strange, either, that my dog in the man-house foreshadowed what I have come to know, or think I know, of my patient and of me. If we can agree that I may have shaped my dog in the man-house after old images of myself on the steps of St. Peter's, and after earlier seated, and unseated, rebellions; and smuggled in various allusions to choices to balk at Peter and to tensions between defiance and compliance and other tensions from my past and my present, I suppose we would agree there is no reason I could not have shaped my image also with regard to my patient's doings past and present, including our current doings with each other. But how does it happen that my image and my patient's dream have so much in common? How does it happen that I see a dog in a high, vaulted, Gothic, churchlike house and my patient dreams of being with a dog in a high, vaulted, Gothic, churchlike house? And how does it happen that his dog in a man-house reminds him of so many of the same tensions in his doings with his father and me as my dog in the man-house had reminded me in regard to my father and him? Even if my patient had borrowed something from my remark that he seemed to feel he was in the dog-house and needed to do something to get into the main house, how can we account for the close similarities of his image and mine, his associations and mine, and for the appeal of the image for each?

We would guess, I suppose, that the moment of the dog in the man-house was one of those moments of knowing more than one knows in more than one sense. At edge-of-awareness, in ways of which I was unaware at center, I must have matched not only our shared tensions, but shared preferences for a particular set of visual arrangements of a particular dog in a particular house to stand for particular tensions and particular configurations of experience and of character of my patient and me.

How could I do this? Am I, then, so very like my patient? I suppose so. We are, it seems to me, very alike. And we are not. The confluences reflected in the dog in the man-house, the associations that lead to and from, the whole process of confluent image-making, I believe, reflect no more than the ordinary, extraordinary likenesses of one person and another, and a little more than the ordinary effort to get at it. I could as easily, and with as much difficulty, have chosen and revealed equally transparent and full, but different, likenesses reflected in other images I have formed with this patient and with others.

The dog in the man-house is no exception. My patient was not uniquely like me, nor point for point like me, by ordinary standards of conflict, background, or character. Each image I have recovered with each patient, no matter how large the differences, has shown its own web of connections and similarities, even if putting it all down might take more time and space than I can manage and more courage than I can muster. As in the case of the dog in the man-house, each image has reflected large similarities in the tensions each was facing and in our shared forms of image-making.

If, at edge-of-awareness, in ways of which at center I was unaware, I matched our mutual preferences for a particular set of visual arrangements of a particular dog in a particular house to stand for particular tensions, intentions, and experiences, I must have been sorting, sifting, selecting, and shaping images, for who knows how long, to fit the content and form of what I had learned of my patient's and my own earlier dreams, waking visual images, metaphors, memories, mannerisms, and more, up to the moment I seemed abruptly to see the dog in the man-house. My patient's remark about the building of the dog-house, and other clues of which

I shall never be aware, must have met a house already —
or almost already — built. I must earlier have thought
and seized chance after chance to learn which images
my patient preferred for telling and hiding what, and
which I preferred, and which we preferred in common.
I must have chosen my image, and my patient's, from
an album of images, both universal and provincial, and
shaped and reshaped it for purposes of which I was but
dimly, if at all, aware.

And my patient, with fewer facts about me than I had
about him, but many more than it might seem, must
have been doing much of the same. When, then, my
patient says something about building a dog-house,
perhaps seeing an image I do not know, and when I say
something about a dog-house and a main house after
seeing an image *he* does not know, and when months
later he dreams of a dog in a man-house (dog and
house both resembling mine), it must be that we have
both been quite canny. Much cannier than we know.

He must have used the model not only of what he had
inferred of my image, but the model of his own that
had been model for mine. And I must have used the
model not only of his image but of my own that were
earlier models for his, and for mine. The images of one
must have shaped the images of the other, in long-drawn-
out exchange. What I saw must have shaped what he
said, must have shaped what I saw and said. And so on.

And on. We must, in more ways than we could know, have arranged with each other exchanges of staggering complexity. The mind boggles. Or it would, if we knew what we were doing.

~ 3

"Why" do I form such images? (I put "why" in quotes to let myself risk a naive teleology and to leave other "why"'s — those of left brain and right, and others — to others.) Are the dog in the man-house, and like images, born of accomplishment? Of disorder? Compassion? Or confusion?

It is hard to think about the act of seeing things without treating it as a wondrous source of inspiration, thereby calling for special measures to guard against disruptive words, or as a breakdown of the ability to think, thereby calling for special measures to clear the seer's head. Though I warn myself not to treat my images as if they were made either in heaven or hell, I find I do regard them as nearer to the former than to the latter.

I seem always to be looking for visual images. I prize them. I count on them to set me straight. I think I see visual images when I am at what I think my best. I see them when I am in a tolerable turmoil: enough but not too much. I see them when complexity seems more challenging than oppressive. Most upset, most at sixes and sevens, most determined to hide my head in what passes for sand, I never see visual images. Never, of course, means hardly ever.

I see my images when I am troubled but not too troubled, puzzled but not too puzzled, startled but not too startled, vexed but not too vexed. I see them most often and most easily when I fall into or can put myself into a slow and steady bobbing from the more awake to the more dreamlike to the more awake to the more dreamlike. Visual images seem to appear, if they appear, when I cross from one to the other. Either way.

I have found that I ignore many images at first, as I did the dog in the man-house, and I think of them, if I think of them at all, as a direct translation of what my patient has said. This illusion of directness and simplicity seems to dull my vigilance. I take it I make this "mistake" because I *wish* to dull my vigilance.*

I have found that I ignore many images because they are near-invisibly brief: a few tenths of a second, I would guess. Others refuse to stay still. They appear,

---

* The parallel could be drawn to coded messages that disguise best if they seem not code but direct statement, and to writing, painting, etc., that conceal symbol, metaphor, allegory, etc., in what seems simple description of "things."

disappear, reappear, grow smaller or larger: part becomes whole, whole becomes part, one shape becomes another, visual image becomes verbal, verbal becomes visual, sometimes words and visual images and whatever else of whichever senses unfold together and one after the other so quickly I cannot keep up. Like the dog in the man-house, they refuse to stay in their place. Any neat scheme, then, of one way of thinking or another is a scheme much neater than life — neater, that is, by far than mine.

I find my images help me to say more than one thing at once: to say one thing, its opposite, and all in the same piece, a composite. I can say dog in the man-house, and man in the dog-house, and, without going through all the steps, can say a dog in a man-house is like a man in a dog-house. I can sketch myself and I can sketch another. I can sketch both at once separately and together. From more than one fix in time and space I can look at more than one thing from more than one fix in time and space. Each image gives form to much I had learned of my patient and myself without knowing I knew it, much I had weighed, compared, contrasted, arranged, and rearranged at center, edge, and farther out of awareness. Each is a vision of more opinion than I knew I opined. Each pulls things together and informs me more quickly than if my ideas and feelings had to be or could be put into words.

But if images help me to go quickly, they also help me to go slowly. They help me to sidle up under cover of ambiguity and to see for a moment — but only for a moment — what is too charged to "speak now in hard words." My images allow me to be tentative and elliptical until I can manage more. They nudge me but do not insist. They whisper what at edge-of-awareness I already believe but at center refuse to admit.

Their virtue, then, is at least double. Service to efficiency and service to timidity coincide. The visual ranges far ahead, scouting what is to come, and to be come upon, while the main body of verbal thinking plods along until, when possible, word catches up with, challenges, corrects, distorts, and augments vision.

~ 4

Do you hear, in my claims for visual images, shrill assertions of the virtue of seeing things? Do you hear counterattacks in advance against charges of mysticism? I cannot help it. If I seem to fear a Philistine whose faith in the word decries all image-making, I hope you will see that the reason lies not in my judgment but in my unease. I lack experience telling *that* I see things, telling *what* I see, and telling *the ways* that I think my

images give me "good advice." (In Shaw's preface to
St. Joan, he asks if Joan's hearing voices means she is
mad, and, on the grounds that her voices give her "good
advice," decides she is not.) If I seem sometimes to pit
cult-of-the-image against cult-of-the-word, it is, I believe,
because I dread being taken for a faddist who promises
relaxation, creativity, and technical proficiency, and because I struggle with old concerns about several kinds
of hubris.

Once, when I was a small boy, four or five, I believe,
out for a walk with my mother, on seeing a dark-bearded
rabbi in a dark hat, I said: "Look. Look. A black Santa
Claus."

It seems I liked pictures then too, especially pictures
for my mother. And my mother, whenever she told of
the incident — she often did — could not hide her
conviction that my image was the image of a poet. She
was too generous, of course. There is no need to compound confusion by calling confusion poetry. "A black
Santa Claus" may have been pre-poetry, or somewhere
in the midground between confusion and poetry, but
surely not poetry.

I don't say the confusion was a simple confusion, if
confusion is ever simple. To the contrary. Months after
I had recalled this incident and had written it down in
these pages, it struck me that I must have been fright-
ened by this apparition and made my peace with the

dark stranger by transforming him into the familiar, the comfortable, and the promising. Still later, I realized that my silver-lining-ism in respect to a dark and intrusive stranger smacked also of an event of my fifth year that took place in the white house and in the climate of the tensions that located the dog in the man-house. Dogs in man-houses, black dogs in white houses, black Santa Clauses, and other Santas, protestant rebellions against papal fathers, show-and-tell for mothers, how hard to see one thing without seeing another.

The midground between confusion and poetry. And I suppose it is so with the dog in the man-house. He is surely not poetry, probably not even full-fledged analogy till I can move him from edge-of-awareness to center, see where I have confused cousin with twin, see the poet's "a lie that tells the truth," and find words to tell that truth to and for myself, and to and for another.

If I claim my images give me good advice, do I then claim for them, and therefore for me, a touch of infallibility? Little boy turned seer? Do I look at my images, and therefore at me, as my mother long ago did, or, more likely, sometimes did, and I wished she would do more? There was a song from the French resistance in World War II in which the hero who has performed wondrous feats of daring and of strength is asked over and over how he has done what he has done. In each refrain, he replies: "In my mother's eyes, I saw only smiles."

If I were to say that each of us relies most on seeing, or hearing, or touching, or tasting, or smelling, or other ways of figuring, if I were to say that each of us prefers those ways he or she has come to, and has no choice but to, trust, if I were to say that in visual ways I happen usually to think best, I would, I believe, have little to retract. I would have said something as incontrovertible as the sign on a Boston apartment complex, "If you lived here, you would be home now."

But I cannot stop at that. I fashion my images, I believe — choose to and have no choice but to — for all those make-believe reasons for which pictures have always been made, in heads and out of. In my images, I play out the pleasures, and pains, of the netherlands of my phantasies, indulge the crudest wishes, the wildest fears, the most mechanical compromises of my early and my continuing childhood. And yet, in these images, I think I do more. I think I try to make virtue out of necessity and necessity out of virtue.

A writer writes, a painter paints, a musician makes music, we all make the images we make, to strike hard and not to strike at all. Each chooses his or her medium both to reveal and to conceal. Each chooses a language that speaks louder and softer than another.

In my images, at edge-of-awareness, in mists of allusion, I see, and avoid seeing, likenesses of my patient and me. In long exchanges of one "dreamer awake" with another, I hide and seek a disguised oneness of myself and another. I preview the grounds on which mutualities might be built; I arrange trial connections before more are tolerable. My visual images, as in the case of the dog in the man-house, are a dare at the crossroads, a moment of readiness to go one way or the other. They are a moment of choice to accept or to reject the almost recognized similarities of myself and the other, and to try or to flee the adventure of fuller mutualities.* I see my images, when I can go either way, but when I am a shade readier to try than to flee.

Between image-making that serves a constructive sense of unity and image-making that arises out of confusion of self and other lies a narrow divide. Without daring that confusion and without exploring that divide, I constrict my vision of self and of other and of the possibilities of reciprocity.

I welcome, therefore, every image I can get my mind's eye on. I try to move my images from edge-of-awareness to center, and I try to follow the lead of my associations (for that, of course, I need words) till I see as much as I can of the likenesses that join my patient and me to each other and to others. Grasping likenesses at center stirs image-making at edge stirs grasp at center. Apollonian joins Dionysian joins Apollonian.

* Fuller, of course, is fuller than yesterday but not full as tomorrow.

Are these images idiosyncracy or are they more? Are they "visual person" analyzing, any person analyzing, or any person, visual or not, analyzing or not?

I think they are each: window to the particular, and window to the general. I think to look to these doings is to look to a commonplace: efforts of each of us to find a common place.

I think we are always sending ourselves evanescent hieroglyphs. Our believing is, in ways from which we never fully depart, always seeing. Our images, whether we recognize them or not, are from our first years and our earliest visions inseparable from and indispensable to our struggles for fuller mutuality, whether we recognize them or not.

VI

In Step and Out

~ 1

MONTHS later, the dog came back.

A patient had gone to see some "couples' skating": "They were good," she says, "but not as good as they used to be.

"The trouble," she says, "is the skaters were slightly out of step."

She tells what was done wrong, and what could have been done right, and of the problems of skating in pairs. She tells of things unconnected — I was sure they were connected but couldn't see how — and then of an argument with a friend who insisted they go to one movie though she would much have preferred another.

"The skaters," I say, "were slightly out of step."

She laughs and nods. She tells then of several times her wishes were not recognized, or, if recognized, overridden. She is full of a growing awareness of a long

belief in her own lowness and others' highness. At the
end of the hour, she recalls a moment long ago — only
one, of course — when the analyst had "insisted, uh, no,
suggested" that in talking of one thing she was avoid-
ing another.

"Really," she says, "I suspect I was not."

For several weeks, she tells of struggles with (?other)
"well-intentioned but misguided" persons — mainly
struggles between herself and men — all of which turn,
over several more weeks, to more bitter struggles of
others, no longer herself, with their mothers.

One day she tells that on the way to her analysis she
had seen in the street a child being dragged by his
mother.

"You can see by her smile," she says, "that she thinks
it's O.K. because she is taking him somewhere for the
child's own good."

After the hour, I resaw my image of the dog in the
man-house. I thought of my father "dragging" me from
one cathedral to another and of other enlightening and
barely endurable experiences to which I'd been taken
for my "own good." I recalled and pictured a series of
children's concerts to which I had been "taken" by my
mother and through which I had fidgeted till the last
passage of the last symphony, when, with hundreds of
other children — could it have been thousands? — I

made a program into an airplane and sailed it high into the air.

The dog in the man-house now changed. The arch of the high doorway in which the dog sat turned into the high arched back of a chair in which I, a child, sat. (A high chair, or a potty chair, or both.) The chair then turned into a porch railing. On the railing sat an infant smiling broadly. In the background, barely visible, was a white house with an arched doorway.

The dog sitting before the high arched doorway of the white man-house, the adolescent sitting on the steps of St. Peter's, the child sitting in the high chair with the arched back, the child sitting in the chair in the high symphony hall, and the infant sitting on the railing before the high arched doorway of the white house seemed at once all of a piece and separate.

Then I saw something else. The infant — now clearly recognizable as me — was not alone. There gazing at me lovingly, smiling gently, and carefully supporting me on my unstable perch, was my mother.*

If the image at first seemed in harmony with the image of the mother in whose eyes I saw only smiles, the harmony was brief. I was struck by a discordant

---

* This image resembles a photograph I have since found, and which I do not recall seeing before but probably saw when a child.

thought: *"This* woman is pushing *this* baby to sit up too soon."

If I had become, or tried to become, remote observer — *"this* woman, *this* baby" — if my thoughts were abstract, my feelings were not. I felt an undertow of rage and grief I know I must have known, but hadn't known I knew, before.

You knew right along that "In My Mother's Eyes" had other refrains. Of course. There is a mother who smiles and a mother who does not. There is a smile that does one thing and a smile that does another. How hard that it is the same smile of the same mother.

∼ 2

WHAT is this last image to which we have now come? Someone seated, something white, porch railing (could it be crib?), high arch (some other curve?). What is vision? What is revision?

If we could see into the depths, would we find in the pictures within pictures the first records of things first seen and imagined? What stays still, or almost still, in the shifting images of the dog sitting before the high arched doorway of the man-house, the youth sitting on the steps before the high arched doorway of St. Peter's, the child sitting on the arched high chair, the older child sitting in the high symphony hall, and the infant sitting on the railing before the white house with the high arched door? Are the coinciding images within images — the constant core of line and shape — faithful reminders and remainders of earliest views of self and of other, self not quite separable from other, and body indistinguishable from nobody? The language must have an alphabet older than we can know.

But if images "contain" traces of the first "syllable of recorded time," they cannot be traces of time unretouched. Neither yesterday nor today can be stored in capsules, nor time in calendars and clocks.

Design must be redesign: yesterday's image shapes today's and today's, yesterday's. The infant who yesterday sat and saw is today the analyst whose occupation and preoccupation is to sit and see. The analyst who sits and sees is predisposed to select, to form, and to reform images of the infant, child, and adolescent who sat and saw. The child is father of the man; the man re-views history to make it his story.

One image shapes and is shaped by the other; all the feelings, urges, and ideas that go with the one, shape and are shaped by all the feelings, urges, and ideas that go with the other. The infant, urged by mother's smiles toward union and division, toward feast and famine, toward company and solitude, toward sit-ups, stand-ups, walkings, talkings, yes-sayings, no-sayings, and other heroic feats, uses images of the mother-in-step when no mother or the mother-out-of-step is there.

Yesterday, before words, images — first blankets and teddy bears of the mind — soothed discords of my first persons and me. But if images soothe, they also stir. If images help me to pretend I have what I miss, how long before they remind me of what is missing?

Today, before words, images help me to explore discords between others and me. They help me to see ways in which, even if somewhat in step, I am always somewhat out. They help me to inquire into my intentions to do for and to others what I believe others have done for and to me: for good and for not so good.

Images help me at last to seek the new mutuality for which another and I are each almost but not quite ready. Mutuality is always the matching of the nearly but not quite ready capacities of two or more persons and is always, therefore, the mutuality of beginners, always both in step and out.

VII

Indirection

~1

A PATIENT begins with a weather report: "It's a *killer* of a storm outside," he says.

He tells of "biting" cold, "fierce" wind, "back-breaking" ice, "record-breaking" snow.

"I need a holiday," he says, "but the company is lousy on taking time off." In petulant tones more sinus than throat he says: "I talked to X yesterday. He's my immediate superior. But he doesn't give a damn. He's just there for the bucks. I talk about taking off, just a week or two, he says no. He couldn't care less. So I ask about a raise. He turns me down flat. He gives me that stuff about pressures from above and the need for economy. They make the big money, and he talks about economy."

He stops. He puts his hands before his eyes. Then he takes them away. He crosses his legs one way. Then he crosses them the other. He clenches his fists. He unclenches.

Then, as if putting an end to the matter, he says: "Well, you know how it is. The rich get richer."

He pauses, then adds: "My grandfather always said that."

"Your grandfather," I say — somewhere between statement and question — "saw no sense in complaining."

"No. He never complained. My grandmother said he let people walk all over him."

He pauses again.

"I guess I'm not too good at speaking up. Even yesterday. I never really told the bastard how pissed I was."

He thinks then of his son who "can't be forced by anyone to do anything he doesn't want." He wonders if his son is "independent" or "defiant," decides he is more independent than defiant, and tells delightedly of several instances.

"You sound as if you wish," I say, "the father were more like the son."

"Yes." He pauses a long pause.

He thinks once more of the "storm outside." He wonders "how bad it might get." He wonders if it will "go on all day." He notices he is feeling "a little nervous." He remembers fears of lightning and thunder when he was five or six. He wonders how he'll feel when he goes "back into the storm." He must "go back," he says, because he is meeting again with his "boss" today.

"Speaking of storms," I say.

He nods. He tells again of his anger at being "used," notices he feels "nervous" again, and then wonders, as if this had been the question all along, whether it's his own storm he fears, or his boss's.

We do not know, of course, exactly what we are inquiring into. We do not deal in exactlies. We see winter storms and other rages, questions of who "makes more" and who "makes less," who "cares" more and who "couldn't care less," who "forces" whom to do what and who "can't be forced," who might "storm" at whom for what. We see dimly where inquiry goes, but exploring, we are always more than a little lost.

He began often with weather reports. In time, he wondered why. We learned of a long-forgotten preoccupation with "nature" at the time of his sister's birth, of a concern with storms of resentment, and with other losses of control, of a delight in being first to know some news when he seemed last to know other, and of a shared weather language with a favorite and favoring uncle whom he hoped the analyst was, or would be, like.

If, in his weather talk, he sometimes avoided what was inside by finding it outside, more often he was not long in finding, within the outside, something inside of which he'd been unaware before. On the whole his inquiries seemed to go better when, having populated the sun, the rain, the fog, the snow, the heat, the wind, or the like with his most stormy or his most pacific feelings, he would then explore, in the outer climate, the intricacies of the inner. If his weather reports postponed other news, they also paved the way. The weather was one of the best barometers of the ongoing inquiries of which he was almost but not quite aware.

How shall we regard such long ways around from inner to outer to inner? Is there a better way? Is there another? Shall we try to make Down Easter into Mediterranean? Or Mediterranean into Down Easter? Shall we judge the microcosms of painters and playwrights and other wrights artful, and all other, artful dodges?

The realist finds the romantic out to sea. The romantic finds the realist stuck in the mud. But each is amphibian. And each, if only we could see how, is always exploring the one world and the other.

~ 2

To see what someone is talking about, to see a "complex," a "pattern," a "process," a "theme," a "flow," or something else I find useful to inquire into, is often easy. But to see what someone — I or another — is already inquiring into, and, in particular, almost but not quite aware of inquiring into, is altogether harder. On a clear day, I cannot see far.

There are the problems I make. There are the problems my patient makes. There are the problems I try to make. There are the problems my patient tries to make. There are the problems we both make without trying. Self inquiries never follow royal roads, but only the shadowy and circuitous.

Each has favorite ways to advance self inquiry. Each has favorite ways to obstruct. What makes our inquiries most perplexing, and fetching, is that our ways of advancing comprise, or convert readily to, our ways of obstructing. Even our most prized ways — maybe especially our most prized — serve the one end as well as the other. In self inquiry, we never find Arcady. We are always, my patient and I, trying both to cultivate and to eradicate the dawning questions of which we are almost but not quite aware.

Susanne Langer once said in a lecture: "People in the decline of inspired eras endlessly take sides on tired old questions instead of pursuing ideas to their further implications. They seek evidence for their beliefs, not new things to think about."

In self inquiry, we are always on the edge between inspired eras and tired old questions. We are always asking questions, always trying to do our questions in. From inspired era to tired old question is but a short step.

At taking the zest out of our most promising questions we are most adept. We are expert deriders, crape-hangers, balancers, legalists, parliamentarians, moralizers, subject-changers, classifiers, cliché-sayers, authority-quoters, anecdotalists, Pollyannas, Cassandras, simplifiers, hyperbolists, chameleons, lotus-eaters, ostriches, mugwumps, and much else. In a pinch, we skillfully cloud large questions in small. ("How many stones are there in that monument?")

Inquiring, we always go back and forth. Simplicity of intent is not to be hoped for. To the contrary. In the realm of self inquiry, when we find our opposing intentions most intense, we know we are where we most belong. When advance becomes retreat becomes advance becomes retreat, challenges and chances for inquiry are fullest.

But if challenges and chances are fullest where inquiries both advance and retreat, those challenges and chances are sometimes fuller than I am ready to meet. When I am unable or unwilling to seek the correspondence of my patient's inquiries and my own, I find I may seek a "higher" ground where I invite inquiry by rule of thumb, average truth, or other rote.

Though I regard such corner-cutting as far from ideal, I do not want to wage war on the rote or the remote which I know I could not get through a day without. Lesser mutualities are often enough, and even when not, as much as I can manage.

If, however, I rely too much on the rote, the rule of thumb, or the otherwise remote, I distract my patient from his or her edge-of-awareness inquiries, and I distract myself from my edge-of-awareness inquiries. And if I intrude so subtly that neither my patient nor I can detect the intrusion — especially if I point to something interesting and useful — I may not only distract us from our ongoing inquiries, but stir the shared delusion that the bit of information we gain is what counts, and what we were, at edge-of-awareness, inquiring into does not.

Is it possible to find something interesting and useful if it does not fit in some way with what we are at edge-of-awareness inquiring into? It would make things simpler if it were not, but unfortunately, it is, I think, possible. We find interesting and useful not only what is unifiable with our edge-of-awareness inquiries, but what is so distant as to be handy for diverting us from them. Especially from our most challenging inquiries.*

If I collude often with my patient in such digression,

---

* Perhaps the pseudoinquiry, or counterinquiry, to which I refer here is close to the accumulating of "dead-knowledge." But knowledge can be vital for some purposes and yet not for advancing edge-of-awareness inquiry; it remains, then, of little use in the making of choices, harmonizing of aims, and informing of acts.

I may not only distract my patient, and me, from our inquiries, but, in time, weaken our ability and will to inquire. And I find I can do the same, if I repeatedly get the words right, but the tune wrong: responding correctly, though unknowingly, to the substance of my patient's inquiry and conveying my mistaken belief that what I am calling attention to, and inviting inquiry into, is what my patient should be inquiring into, but is not.

The way, then, is strewn with obstacles. By my patient. And me. That's the nature of our enterprise. When my patient talks weather talk, we each want to listen and we each want not. We want not because we think the weather talk is small talk, and because we know it is not. And I want to listen and not because when I learn more about my patient's weather talk I learn more about my own. Even if less a weather person than my patient, I find I am more a weather person than I knew. Seeing our inquiries, we see only a little, and less, directly. To see which way the wind blows we watch tiny flutterings of mood and mind, as the sailor, looking straight ahead, watches the telltale, high on the mast and at the upper edge of the eye.

~

~ 3

WHEN things go well, trouble notwithstanding, my patient and I manage to advance our individual inquiries and to match some parts of those inquiries one with the other. We match some agendas of inquiry. We match some ways of inquiring. And we advance the mutualities that come of the shared struggle to advance and to match our inquiries in the face of our joint intentions to disrupt.

I need my self inquiry to help advance my patient's and my patient's to help advance my own. In the fugues of self inquiry, solos are surprisingly hard to sustain.

We need each other to serve our edge-of-awareness efforts to inquire and to develop our means of inquiring; and we need each other to serve a peculiar requirement of focus. We advance our edge-of-awareness inquiries most successfully when we focus on something else at center. We see better at edge than at center. What we see at center helps us to find what we are looking for at edge because what we see at center is what we are looking for at edge. I wish I could see things more simply but I cannot.

My best seeing is inside out. I inquire best into myself when I seem to be inquiring into my patient and I inquire best into my patient when I seem to be inquiring into myself. I need my self inquiry to help advance my patient's and my patient's to help advance my own. My patient has his weather in which he sees himself; and I have mine. My weather is largely my patient.*

And if my patient's self inquiry is to help me with my own and my own with my patient's, our inquiry must be up-to-date. Last month's or last week's won't do. Memories for inquiry are brief, the period of contagion even briefer. For a day or two, and sometimes less, having learned something of my patient's inquiry or my own, I am moved as we are moved when having come lately upon a new idea, new word, or new thing, we come upon it so often and in such a clear and ramifying view, we find it hard to believe that what is now so common was before so rare.

One inquiry helps with another and another. In the business of self inquiry we need all the help we can get. The dog in the man-house led me with the help of one patient to one smile of my mother; and the dog in the man-house revisited led me, with the help of the other patient, to another.

My patient needs my help; I need my patient's. If it

---

* If I, and analysts in general, may be persons who need inquiries of others to advance their own, I think we are in this regard like others, if a little more so.

can be said it is the analyst's job to help in the advance of the patient's ongoing inquiry, it can as well be said the patient's job is to aid in the advance of the analyst's.

Does it sound odd to talk this way? Why? Because the patient has asked for help and the analyst has not? Is asking, then, a license to get without giving? Or is it odd to talk of the patient's job when it is the analyst who is paid? Is money, then, the only real pay?

Or is the issue that the analyst is expert, healthy, and wise, and the patient is not? Surely this is not only an invidious but a dubious distinction.

We seem to insist on regarding the analyst as some sort of parent, and a very odd sort at that. A selfless server? Automaton?

How awful if we could really be served by someone who is, seems, or purports to be selfless. "Please, Ma, do me a favor. Don't do me any more favors."

There is a statue on the Boston Esplanade upon the pedestal of which is engraved, in Latin, of course, "Not for myself, but for my country." Nineteenth century, of course. The things politicians say so as not to seem self-serving. The things politicians say to hide (and to tell) that the self-serving they have in mind (the only self-serving of which they can conceive?) is self-serving at the expense of others. Is false other-ism the cure for false self-ism? Or part of the same disease?

"Not for myself, but for my country." What kind of country is then served, the good of which is not good for myself? And which myself is the good of my country not good for?

VIII

The Moment

~1

As an analysis advances, inquiry becomes more insistent and consistent, and directions clearer. And though I do not remark directly on my inquiry but only on my patient's, my patient knows — without dwelling on it — that the comments and questions of the commentator and questioner reveal at least as much about the commentator and questioner as about the one commented on and questioned. Through my patient's efforts, then, and mine, our edge-of-awareness inquiries are made more and more coincident.

As an analysis advances, I begin to see more clearly our synchronous inquiries into synonymous tensions between urges toward mutualities and urges at odds with or indifferent to them. My patient and I struggle now separately and now in concert to make the contrary, the divergent, and the indifferent into the coexistent, the harmonious, and, when we can, the synergistic. Our inquiries gradually reveal and embrace the shared hidden agendas of harmony and of hope — and therefore of health — that have brought my patient and me to our combined endeavor.

Reconsider the moment of the dog:

Though inquiries are restless in category, one flowing quickly into another, it became increasingly apparent, to my patient and me, that he was increasingly inquiring at edge-of-awareness, and sometimes at center, into expanded possibilities of dissension and of opposition. Civil and uncivil. My patient was inquiring over and over into mutually advantageous ways to disagree with and to oppose now one person and now another. Especially me. After long adhering to mutualities of forced amiability ("apples for the teacher," "gifts," and "tricks"), and having long been short on mutualities of dissent, he seemed now to envision and (almost) to assay more. After months of inquiry into old confusions of assertion and attack, and old confusions of declaration and demand, inquiry into persistent illusions of power and paralysis, and inquiry into hot rages, affections, and fears of which he'd long been ashamed, he seemed now on the verge of new ways to assert both his affections and disaffections. He was poised to spring from the dog-house of customary uncooperative compliance.

All this was salient: on the one hand, a constricted and constricting generosity that demanded similar gifts in return (and back and forth), and, on the other, a growing urge toward more fruitful accord born of candid, direct, spontaneous, and more prepared discord.*

All this, together with old conflicts "within" himself and old battles with his father and others, he was now recreating in doings with me, in this moment of the dog in the man-house.

Recreating? Reliving? Repeating? Recapitulating? If nature does not repeat herself exactly — still less in matters such as these — what can I mean to say if I say he, I, or anyone recreates?

Does recreating mean confusing? Maybe. Confusion, I suppose, is never far off when past is made, more vividly than usual, present. And yet I don't want to say he or you or I am only being childish any more than we are only being adultish.

If I say my patient was confusing me with others, I want to give the confusion its due. His confusion was a careful confusion.

For months, he set the stage for the re-creations his inquiries required. For months he sought and found the

---

* Not that he was like an old dog learning new tricks — that, after all, was part of the problem — but he was striving to do what he had done only rarely before, and trying to inquire into all that stood, and that he placed, in his way.

particular sights, sounds, smells, and all else he needed to evoke, give form, and make plausible the feelings he was almost but not quite aware of inquiring into. He chose aspects of my height, shape, and gait, a low "comforting" tone here, a higher "scolding" tone there, a few of my opening and closing "smiles" and "frowns" (two of the former and more of the latter), a whiff of tobacco from the pipe he imagined I smoked between hours (the smell of smoke kindly supplied by an earlier patient), to which he added some references I had made over the years to baseball, the rudder of a boat, a boy, and a book, a few patches of blue (my eyes, a shirt, and a glimpse of the sky from my office window seemed nicely to do), the low ceiling of the room, a bookcase, a desk, and a chair, mentally rearranged.

If the conditions had demanded he use different particulars to cast me in the role his inquiries needed, I am confident he would, with comparable skill, have found other and equally convincing signs of the identity of his father and me.

In the conversion of past to present, he did not merely react. He scanned, he selected, he set aside, he resurrected, he arranged, he rearranged, till he had made a portrait of me of a kind we would probably call accurate, superimposed on a portrait of his father the accuracy of which we have no reason to doubt. Of gross distortion and careless confusion he seemed to have little need. He accomplished his ends by a deft lowering of one threshold here and the raising of another there. We find blue when we are looking for it. And blue with smell of smoke is different from blue without.

The past he recreated was steeped in present purpose. The present was ordered small step by small step until at last search and possibility met halfway. And, having cast me in the needed role, he began often and persuasively to invite me both to accept and to reject his trick-performing and gift-bearing.

In carefully sought and chosen moments — the spur of the moment long and well sharpened — an inquirer pursues, and must pursue, his or her inquiry in regard to another and must live out a piece of that inquiry with that other. Some work more in bold color. Some prefer arrangement in gray. Bold, gray, high- or low-key, inquiry must at last be real-ized: made "real," felt, and seen in the round.

There comes a moment — the dramatic are the ordinary, magnified — when an inquirer wishes, and is impelled, to make inquiry into immediacy, view into rendezvous. Beyond the ordinary and seemingly sporadic harmonics of subject and style, beyond ordinary resonances of what is inquired into and how, there arise key junctures of intensity and longevity, networks of such range, color, complexity, and power, that we sense or imagine the inquirer has been driven, and is driving, to compose a new order of repetition and re-creation. Here, he or she composes and is composed by earlier barely dreamed, and undreamed, harmonies.

Inside psychoanalysis, as out, when we manage to arrange such moments, our aims seem a mix of the conservative-reactionary and the conservative-progressive. We reopen old questions and close them. We bring forth old answers and change them. Inquiries bring us, and we bring them, over and over, to moments of large choice: to hold to the old or opt for the new, and how much and how to blend one with the other.

These are moments of blind and blinding repetition that put the lid on inquiry.* These are moments of realization that renew inquiry. And sometimes we do not need to repeat the past at all, or very little, but, catching it on the wing when repetition is impulse rather than act, we move inquiry at once from the past to a larger and more promising re-creation. Sometimes. But not often. Mostly, we do a bit of everything.

These moments of reliving, repeating, realizing, and recreating for my patient are similar moments for me. In the moment of the dog in the man-house, in a shift of tone here, a figure of speech there, a thought and feeling about my patient, a thought and feeling about

---

* If never exact repetition, they are in some ways close enough to look so, and driven enough to replace rather than stir recollection, and to disrupt rather than advance inquiry.

me, a quickening of interest, a delay, a comment to him, a failure to comment, I found myself in the midst of my past, in some ways as my father, in some, as son. And, like my patient, I struggled between old urges to a forced accord and new urges to a mutually liberating discord. I was faced with ways I had colluded with my patient to blur borders between cooperation and conciliation. I was faced with my own tendencies toward trick-performing and gift-bringing, and the welcoming of them in others.

Though it is better as a rule that some of my reliving be a shade more forward-looking where my patient's may be a shade more backward-looking, and better that some of the consensual conflicts of my character be less central and compelling, nothing happens to the one, I find, without something similar happening to the other. I find it, that is, if I look carefully.

Such moments of parallelism of my patient and me might be regarded as — might be — a special disorder. They can surely cause trouble. But when, on looking carefully, I can find no signs at all of such parallelism, I find we are in greater trouble.

"In the mind of one man is the whole world." I might as well face it. What better can I do? My patient and I seem in greater trouble when I am most clear that it is only my patient who is confused, and only I not.

What I find, when I am up for the finding, is that

my patient and I not only inquire into similar dilemmas of mutuality but, in moments mutually arranged, we both relive old truths and old fictions, and both struggle to compound them with new: both, that is, struggle between intentions to stay as we are and to change into what we wish we could be.*

Without joint disorder we make little order, and less progress. When our self inquiries meet, join, and mingle in shared repetition and optimal turmoil, when maintenance and metamorphosis seem to vie — till we find ways they do not — these are the moments of the most radical possibility. For my patient and for me. "The best of times and the worst of times." In these moments, the dare at the crossroads is double.

~ 2

EACH art, the "Art" we call by that name, and the other arts of living, has its own idiom — medium and means — by which "outer" tensions can be conceived and

---

* I do not suggest there is or should be an identity in form or intensity of my patient's reactions and mine, nor that the mixing of two disorders in *folie à deux* will magically benefit one or the other, but that I find my patient always struggles with universal and never fully solved problems; there is always a lively counter-part in me; it is better that the counter-part be accessible to my attention.

made consonant with "inner." Each art provides a medium and means by which moments of high possibility are gradually and laboriously arranged; in these moments, "inner" and "outer" tensions are recreated and brought into fuller accord. For each art, aesthetic is always synaesthetic.

Each artist struggles to make harmonious those "inner" and "outer" tensions conceivable and manageable by that medium and means, in the current state of that art, consonant with the artist's tensions, conceivable and manageable in the current state of the artist's evolving capacities. The inquiry into the "inner" world is always the inquiry into the "outer"; the one world *is* the other.*

To see and do what we want, we must mostly see and do analogues. Mutualities cannot be manufactured or mass-produced; they must be created and recreated anew.

Mutualities do not grow in straight lines but spirals. The spirals are shaped — natured and nurtured — in an expanding field of urges for and against. We cannot directly arrange these large moments we and another

---

* It might be an attractive, if difficult, task to examine the built-in ground plan in the evolution of social mutualities and to compare it with the built-in ground plan in the evolution of parallel mutualities — the problems of consonance, dissonance, innovation, discipline, individuality, etc. — in one or another of the "Arts."

need. They are arranged indirectly by ourselves *and* the other. If we try to make experiences directly corrective, they are more likely to be incorrect.*

Sticking to the pursuit of our inquiries, we are apt, in passing, to advance the moments we need to advance mutualities. Trying to contrive these moments, we are apt to obstruct. We cannot contrive, force, or speed. In Italy they say: *"Partito, ma non arrivato."* Departed but not arrived. On the way. That is especially the way of mutualities. There is no rushing. They must come in their own bittersweet time; we saunter on the long way around. And, fortunately, since each step of each person on the path recreates the steps that came before and anticipates those to come, we are never too far from each other, whatever ground each covers, and whichever seems how close or how far ahead or behind.

In the moments of highest possibility — not arrangeable, yet arranged — what we learn from the pursuit of our inquiries, what we learn about new ways to inquire, and what we learn from what we experience in the learning and in the trying to learn, all work together in new unities of idea and experience, of past and present, and of self and other. Inquiry advances the

---

* Woodrow Wilson once said — and there is reason to believe he knew what he was saying — "The man who sets out directly to be good only succeeds in making himself obnoxious."

moments of possibility; and inquiry, persisted in, urges possibility toward probability.

Outside psychoanalysis as inside, each person tries, through his or her special medium and means, to inquire into large questions of mutuality and tries, in nodal moments, both to preserve old answers and to find better.* Each searches repeatedly for someone or something with whom or with which to live out, in these moments, the lead questions with which he or she is now concerned. We seek stability. We seek change. We are sessile. We are restless.

Do we "intend" change? Does the acorn "intend" oakdom? The panda, a thumb?

In September of 1982, it no longer seems strange to ponder the possibility, or probability, that the urge to recreate old mutualities and to create newer and fuller, in expanding spirals of critical moments, is analogue to — reverberation of? — the tendency of all living matter, and (if, as I have heard say, three laws of thermodynamics are not enough) the tendency of all nonliving too, to enter into larger and more and more unified relation to what was, or seemed, its surround. In fact, it becomes now harder and harder to conceive of any development, human biological (physical-psycho-

---

* "The farmer is not only farming, but *man* farming." Sometimes.

logical-social, political-historical), general biological, or inanimate, that does not comprise an intention, a thrust, a tendency, not only toward the atomic but as well, and in tension with it, an intention, a thrust, a tendency toward the molecular. Viewed so, the small eddy we call human mutuality, and its innate and cultured tendency in critical moments to spread, becomes an eddy of that larger tendency — not alone accident or "practical" need — toward the molecular.* Viewed so, each window becomes, more and more decidedly, window to the world.

---

* Of this, the moments analysts call "transference" may be a small constructive and obstructive piece.

IX

The Field before You

Having finished the last chapter the day before, loaded my camera the night before, and risen early when the light was right, I walked one day through airy woods to a spot high on a headland — "all America is behind me now" — where months before I'd conceived the idea to depict a broad, uninterrupted view of the sea. The delay between idea and act was only partly a lack of earlier opportunity, but also, I believe, a vague and preliminary honoring of a principle I've since grasped more firmly. Whenever I want most to make a picture — film or paint — of a compelling scene (the more compelling require it more), the picture goes better if, for a year or more, when I revisit the scene, I forget my camera or brush. When I finally bring the needed tools and settle to the intended task, the picture then seems consistently to photograph or to paint itself. I take it that in the gap between intention and execution, out of view of the scene, freer of it, and having time to review and rework it, I photograph or paint the picture in the back of my head, where vision is clearer and fuller.*

Having made my way back at last to the panoramic scene I had meant to portray — this time with camera — I realized at once what I must already have known: the camera is a poor instrument for pursuing panoramas — at least my camera, since I have neither a wide-angle lens nor, lacking it, the tripod and the patience wanted to take a lot of little pictures and to fit them into one. I undertook, therefore, after some wandering about, a shift from the broad view to the long. I made pictures mainly of foreground grasses, shrubs, and dune, middle-ground beach, and in the distance a little sky, and less ocean; the ocean now a remote flag of indigo with two or three tiny streaks of foam from waves just broken on sandy shore. It seemed, at last, the best picture of the ocean was one of something else — or almost of something else.

Circling now to the lee of the dune, looking for another vista to the sea, musing vaguely about the contrast between the vast I'd intended and the touch I'd

---

* When lacking time, or not taking it, to do things right, I find the best I can do is to look at the scene through a very dark glass, so that, seeing some things less, I see others more. This, I suppose, is part of the general necessity to court the conditions in which those accidents are likely to occur of which we mean to take advantage.

taken, I decided that since I seemed to be trying to see if a little was better than more, I'd carry the experiment further. I decided a better picture of the sea might be a picture of a characteristic path away from it, a path such as the one on which I was now walking.

I took it: a curve of sand with tufts of grass struggling on the crown in an onshore breeze, and on each side small stands of stunted and twisted oaks and pines so trimmed by easterly winds, all might have been chosen, shaped, and arranged to be a Japanese garden. I came, then, upon a smaller picture waiting to be pictured close up. A step to the side of the road, lit by a low shaft of still-early sunlight, were three blackberries, two not quite ripe, nestled in saw-toothed leaves, with smoother bayberry to one side and on the other a piece of the rough gray-brown of the trunk of a pine. Turning my camera from one angle to another, I wrestled with the vexing problem of how to picture, in pleasing proximity, berries, leaves, and pine, without recording a small piece of string tied so tightly around the trunk I could not undo it, and not having a knife, could not cut it, which insistently intruded a foreign chrome green and a horizontal line at odds with the verticals I wanted.

I must have begun then to wonder why anyone would have tied a string there. I say "I must" because I was unaware of any thoughts except how to make a picture of the berries by the side of the road leading away from the sea. Yet, suddenly, in seeming answer to the question I did not know I was asking, I realized the offending string was intended to mark a berry patch much larger than the one I had seen. Turning, now, from photos to berries, I saw immediately the substantial patch I had seemed neither to have seen nor sought. (Only later did it occur to me that I had known right along that this is the sort of place blackberries grow and the time of year they ripen.)

Looking to make a picture of the ocean in a way I did not know I was looking, *and* preoccupied with correspondences of large to small, large worlds in small, small dog in large man-house and other small figures in large, and tendencies of things small to evolve into things larger, I shrunk an ocean from large to small and pushed it from near to far. Pursuing my vision of an ocean to a few small berries, I tried to remove the indicator that seemed intruder and then found, behind the small, the large patch of berries for which I did not know I was looking.*

Inner to inner, inner to outer, outer to outer, and outer to inner, we find what we are looking for. We cannot do else. We find the scenes we have already seen. Each view is a minority view looking for another.

---

* The corresponding inner world for which I selected, arranged, and rearranged this outer, is not hard to guess a piece of, but I shall leave that for another, a newer, and a braver day.

Always seeing double — inside and out — our view is always singular.

Once when one of my children was very small — two, going on three, I think — he woke up screaming in the night. He cried: "Billy fell down the drain, Billy fell down the drain." I turned on the lights and showed Billy snug in his bed, proving Billy not in the drain. I carefully explained, on several grounds, the differences between fact and dream. My son happily concurred that his brother's fall was dream, not fact. The next day, I heard him say as the two boys stood by a sink, "Watch out, Billy. Remember what almost happened last night."

We find what we are looking for. We cannot do else. Mutualities of ends shape mutualities of means shape mutualities of ends. Moment leads to moment leads to moment.

"The field that you are standing before appears to have the same proportions as your own life."